Downwood, Claverton Down Road, Bath BA2 6DT

First published 1994


Acknowledgements:
Illustrated by Charles Robinson
Edited by Walter Jerrold
Printed in Malaysia

# My Book of Fairy Tales

## Volume 2

# INTRODUCTION

ALL the best fairy-tales seem to be the old ones. The stories that entranced the childhood of our parents are still the favourites, though the manner of their telling has altered. Further, it may be said that the best nursery tales are told in a universal language. If only his story is worthy, it ensures the teller the freedom of the nursery everywhere.

Could the story-tellers represented in this volume be assembled to lead, in a Grand Nursery Pageant, their Princes and Princesses, Ogres and

# INTRODUCTION

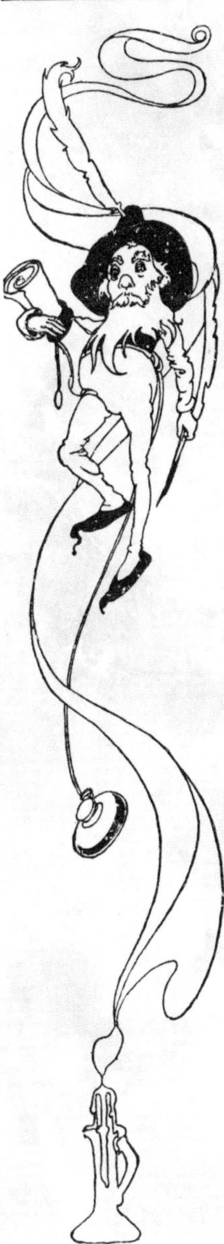

Fairies, what a varied spectacle it would be! Perhaps the place of honour would be given to the old Oriental who collected the tales of the *Arabian Nights*, and who would bring with him the far-travelled Sindbad. They would be followed by a Frenchman, Charles Perrault, with a delightful group including Blue Beard, Beauty, and the Beast. Dear Hans Andersen would present the Ugly Duckling and the Little Tin Soldier, and our own Robert Southey would have his hands full in charge of the Three Bears. As for Cinderella and Rumpelstiltskin, it would be hard to decide who should escort them, for under different names they play their part in the nursery romances of several countries.

Besides the celebrities would be strangers whose very names are unknown to us, but with whom we have long wanted to be friends. Amongst such anonymous authors we should see the story-tellers to whom we owe the histories of Dick Whittington and of the two famous Jacks—the Giant Killer and the proprietor of the Beanstalk.

What a welcome they would have wherever there are children, and grown-ups who have kept a young corner in their hearts!

These story-tellers are the true magicians: they can open the door between the nursery and fairyland.

# CONTENTS

# Dick Whittington and His Cat

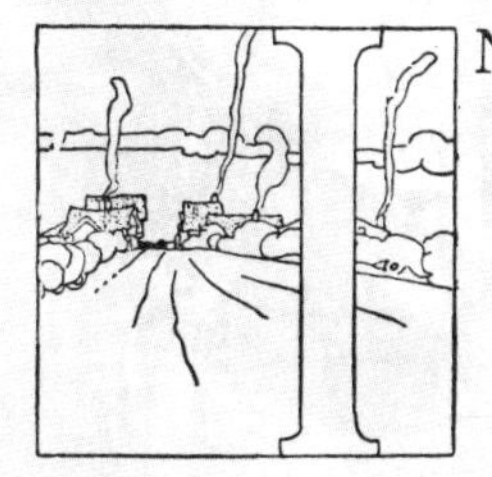

IN the reign of Edward the Third there was a poor orphan boy, named Dick Whittington, living in a country village a long way from London. He was a sharp little lad, and the stories that he heard, of London being paved with gold, made him long to visit that city.

One day, a large wagon and eight horses, with bells at their heads, drove through the village. Dick thought it must be going to London, so he asked the wagoner to let him walk by the side of the wagon. As soon as the wagoner heard that poor Dick had neither father nor mother, and saw by his ragged clothes that he could not be worse off than he was, he told him he might go if he would; so they set off together.

Dick got safely to London, and was in such a hurry to see the fine streets paved with gold, that he ran through many of them, thinking every moment to come to those that were paved with gold; for Dick had seen a guinea three times in his own little village, and remembered what a deal of money it brought in change; so he thought he had nothing to do but to take up some little bits of the pavement, and he would then have as much money as he could wish for. Poor Dick ran till he was tired, and had quite forgotten his friend the wagoner. At last, finding it grow dark, and that every way he turned he saw nothing but dirt instead of gold, he sat down in a dark corner, and cried himself to sleep. Next morning, being very hungry, he got up and walked about, and asked everybody he met to give him a halfpenny to keep him from starving. At last, a good-natured-looking gentleman saw how hungry he looked.

"Why don't you go to work, my lad?" said he.

"I would," answered Dick, "but I do not know how to get any."

"If you are willing," said the gentleman, "come with me;" and so saying, he took him to a hayfield, where Dick worked briskly, and lived merrily till the hay was all made. After this, he found himself as badly off as before; and being almost starved again, he laid himself down at the door of Mr. Fitzwarren, a rich merchant. Here the cook-maid, an ill-tempered creature, called out to poor Dick:

"What business have you there, you lazy rogue? If you do not take yourself away, we will see how you will like a sousing of some dish-water I have here, that is hot enough to make you jump."

At this time, Mr. Fitzwarren himself came home to dinner; and when he saw a dirty ragged boy lying at the door, he said:

"Why do you lie there, my lad? you seem old enough to work; I am afraid you are lazy."

"No, sir," said Dick to him. "I would work with all my heart; but I do not know anybody, and I am sick for want of food."

"Poor fellow!" answered Mr. Fitzwarren; "get up, and let me see what ails you."

Dick tried to rise, but was too weak to stand, for he had not eaten anything for three days. So the kind merchant ordered him to be taken into the house, and have a good dinner given to him; and to be kept to do what dirty work he could for the cook. Dick would have lived happily in this good family, if it had not been for the ill-natured cook, who was finding fault and scolding him from morning till night; and besides, she was so fond of basting, that, when she had no roast meat to baste, she would be basting poor Dick. But though the cook was so ill-tempered, the footman was quite different. He had lived in the family many years, and was an elderly man, and very kind-hearted. He had once a little son of his own, who died when about the age of Dick; so he could not help feeling pity for the poor boy, and sometimes gave him a halfpenny to buy gingerbread or a top. The footman was fond of reading, and used often in the evening to entertain the other servants with some amusing book. Little Dick took pleasure in hearing this good man, which made him wish very much to learn to read too; so the next time the footman gave him a halfpenny, he bought a little book with it; and with the footman's help, Dick soon learnt his letters, and afterwards to read.

About this time, Miss Alice, Mr. Fitzwarren's daughter, was going out one morning for a walk, and Dick was told to put on a suit of good clothes that Mr. Fitzwarren gave him, and walk behind her. As they went, Miss Alice saw a poor woman with one child in her arms, and another on her back. She pulled out her purse and gave the woman some money; but as she was putting it into her pocket again, she dropped it on the ground, and walked on. It was lucky that Dick was behind, and saw what she had done; so he picked up the purse, and gave it to her again. Another time, when Miss Alice was sitting with the window open and amusing herself with a favourite parrot, it suddenly flew away to the branch of a high tree, where all the servants were afraid to venture after it. As soon as Dick heard of this, he pulled off his coat, and climbed up the tree as nimbly as a squirrel; and after a great deal of trouble, caught her and brought her down safely to his mistress. Miss Alice thanked him, and liked him ever after for this. The ill-humoured cook was now a little kinder; but, besides this, Dick had another hardship to get over. His bed stood in a garret, where there were so many holes in the floor and the walls, that every night he was waked in his sleep by the rats and mice, which ran over his face, and made such a noise that he sometimes thought the walls were tumbling down about him. One day, a gentleman who came to see

Mr. Fitzwarren required his shoes to be cleaned; Dick took great pains to make them shine, and the gentleman gave him a penny. With this he thought he would buy a cat; so the next day, seeing a little girl with a cat under her arm, he went up to her, and asked if she would let him have it for a penny. The girl said she would, and that it was a very good mouser. Dick hid the cat in the garret, and always took care to carry a part of his dinner to her; and in a short time he had no more trouble from the rats and mice. Soon after, his master had a ship ready to sail; and as he thought it right all his servants should have some chance for good fortune as well as himself, he called them into the parlour, and asked them what they would send out. They all had something that they were willing to venture, except poor Dick, who had neither money nor goods. For this reason he did not come into the parlour with the rest; but Miss Alice guessed what was the matter, and ordered him to be called in. She then said she would lay down some money for him from her own purse; but her father told her this would not do, for Dick must send something of his own. When poor Dick heard this, he said he had nothing but a cat.

"Fetch your cat then, my good boy," said Mr. Fitz-warren, "and let her go."

Dick went upstairs and brought down poor puss, and gave her to the captain, with tears in his eyes. All the company laughed at Dick's odd venture; and Miss Alice, who felt pity for the poor boy, gave him some halfpence to buy another cat.

This, and other marks of kindness shown him by Miss Alice, made the ill-tempered cook jealous of poor Dick; and she began to use him more cruelly than ever, and always made game of him for sending his cat to sea. She asked if he thought his cat would sell for as much money as would buy a stick to beat him. At last, poor Dick could not bear this any longer, and thought he would run away from his place; so he packed up his few things, and set out very early in the morning on the first of November. He walked as far as Highgate, and there sat down on a stone, which to this day is called Whittington's stone, and began to think which road he should take farther. While he was thinking what he should do, the bells of Bow Church began to ring, and he fancied their sounds seemed to say:

"Turn again, Whittington,
Lord Mayor of London."

"Lord Mayor of London!" said he to himself. "Why, to be sure I would put up with almost anything now, to be Lord Mayor of London, and ride in a fine coach, when I grow to be a man! I will go back and think nothing of the cuffing and scolding of the old cook, if I am to be Lord Mayor of London at last."

Dick went back, and was lucky enough to get into the house and set about his work before the cook came down.

The ship, with the cat on board, was a long time at sea; and was at last driven by the winds on a part of the coast of Barbary. The people came in great numbers to see the sailors, and treated them very civilly; and when they became better acquainted, were eager to buy the fine things with which the ship was laden. When the captain saw this, he sent patterns of the best things he had to the king of the country; who was so much pleased with them, that he sent for the captain and the chief mate to the palace. Here they were placed, as is the custom of the country, on rich carpets, marked with gold and silver flowers. The King and Queen were seated at the upper end of the room; and a number of dishes, of the greatest rarities, were brought in for dinner; but, before they had been on the table a minute, a vast number of rats and mice rushed in, and helped themselves from every dish. The captain wondered at this, and asked if these vermin were not very unpleasant.

"Oh, yes!" they said, "and the King would give half his riches to get rid of them; for they not only waste his dinner, as you see, but disturb him in his bedroom, so that he is obliged to be watched while he is asleep."

The captain was ready to jump for joy when he heard this. He thought of poor Dick's cat, and told the King he had a creature on board his ship that would kill all the rats and mice. The King was still more glad than the captain.

"Bring this creature to me," said he, "and if it can do what you say, I will give you your ship full of gold for her."

The captain, to make quite sure of his good luck, answered, that she was such a clever cat for catching rats and mice, that he could hardly bear to part with her; but that to oblige His Majesty he would fetch her.

"Run, run!" said the Queen, "for I long to see the creature that will do such a service."

Away went the captain to the ship, while another dinner was got ready. He came back to the palace soon enough to see the table full of rats and mice again, and the second dinner likely to be lost in the same way as the first. The cat did not wait for bidding, but jumped out of the captain's arm, and in a few moments laid almost all the rats and mice dead at her feet. The rest, in a fright, scampered away to their holes.

The King and Queen were charmed to get so easily rid of such a plague. They desired that the creature might be brought for them to look at. On this, the captain called out: "Puss, puss!" and the cat ran and jumped upon his knee. He then held her out to the Queen, who was afraid to touch a creature that was able to kill so many rats and mice; but when she saw how gentle the cat seemed, and how glad she was at being stroked by the captain, she ventured to touch her too, saying all the time: "Poot, poot," for she could not speak English. At last the Queen took puss on her lap, and by degrees became quite free with her, till puss purred herself to sleep. When the King had seen the actions of mistress puss, and was told that she would soon have young ones, which might in time kill all the rats and mice in his country, he bought the captain's whole ship's cargo; and afterwards gave him a great deal of gold besides, which was worth still more, for the cat. The captain then took leave, and set sail with a fair wind, and arrived safe at London.

One morning, when Mr. Fitzwarren had come into the counting house, and seated himself at the desk, somebody came tap, tap, tap, at the door.

"Who is there?" asked Mr. Fitzwarren.

"A friend," answered someone; and who should it be but the captain, followed by several men carrying vast iumps of gold, that had been paid him by the King of Barbary for the ship's cargo. They then told the story of the cat, and showed the rich present that the King had sent to Dick for her; upon which the merchant called out to his servants:

"Go fetch him, we will tell him of the same;
Pray call him Mr. Whittington by name."

Mr. Fitzwarren now showed himself a really good man, for while some of his clerks said so great a treasure was too much for such a boy as Dick, he answered:

"God forbid that I should keep the value of a single penny from him! It is all his own, and he shall have every farthing's worth of it."

He sent for Dick, who happened to be scouring the cook's kettles, and was quite dirty; so that he wanted to excuse himself from going to his master. Mr. Fitzwarren, however, made him come in, and ordered a chair to be set for him, so that poor Dick thought they were making game of him, and began to beg his master not to play tricks with a poor boy, but to let him go again to his work.

"Indeed, Mr. Whittington," said the merchant, "we are all in earnest with you; and I heartily rejoice in the news these gentlemen have brought you; for the captain has sold your cat to the King of Barbary, and brought you, in return for her, more riches than I possess; and I wish you may long enjoy them!"

Mr. Fitzwarren then told the men to open the great treasure they had brought with them, and said:

"Mr. Whittington has now nothing to do but to put it in some place of safety."

Poor Dick hardly knew how to behave himself for joy. He begged his master to take what part of it he pleased, since he owed it all to his kindness.

"No, no," answered Mr. Fitzwarren, "this is all your own; and I have no doubt you will use it well."

Dick next asked his mistress, and then Miss Alice, to accept a part of his good fortune, but they would not; and at the same time told him that his success afforded them great pleasure. But the poor fellow was too kind-hearted to keep it all to himself; so he made a handsome present to the captain, the mate, and every one of the sailors, and afterwards to his good friend the footman, and the rest of Mr. Fitzwarren's servants; and even to the ill-natured cook. After this, Mr. Fitzwarren advised him to get himself dressed like a gentleman; and told him he was welcome to live in his house till he could provide himself with a better.

When Whittington's face was washed, his hair curled, his hat cocked, and he was dressed in a nice suit of clothes, he was as handsome and genteel as any young man who visited at Mr. Fitzwarren's; so that Miss Alice, who had been so kind to him, and thought of him with pity, now looked upon him as fit to be her sweetheart; and the more so, no doubt, because Whittington was now always thinking what he could do to oblige her, and making her the prettiest presents that could be. Mr. Fitzwarren soon saw their love for each other, and proposed to join them in marriage; and to this they both readily agreed. A day for the wedding was soon fixed; and they were attended to church by the Lord Mayor, the Court of Aldermen, the Sheriffs, and a great number of the richest merchants in London, whom they afterwards treated with a very fine feast.

History tells us that Mr. Whittington and his lady lived in great splendour, and were very happy. They had several children. He was Sheriff of London in the year 1360, and several times afterwards Lord Mayor: the last time, he entertained King Henry the Fifth, on His Majesty's return from the famous Battle of Agincourt. In this company, the King, on account of Whittington's gallantry, said:

"Never had prince such a subject;" and when Whittington was told this at the table, he answered:

"Never had subject such a king."

Going with an address from the city, on one of the King's victories, he received the honour of knighthood. Sir Richard Whittington supported many poor; he built a church, and also a college, with a yearly allowance to poor scholars, and near it raised a hospital. The figure of Sir Richard Whittington, with his cat in his arms, carved in stone, was to be seen till the year 1780, over the archway of the old prison of Newgate, that stood across Newgate Street.

# The Goose Girl

N old widowed Queen had a beautiful daughter betrothed to a Prince who lived far away. As the time drew near for her to be married, she got ready to set off on her journey to his country. The Queen packed up many costly things—jewels, and gold, and silver; trinkets, fine dresses, everything that became a royal bride, for she loved her child very dearly; and she gave her a waiting-maid to ride with her, and each had a horse for the journey. The Princess's horse was called Falada, and it could speak.

When the time came for them to set out, the old Queen went into her bedchamber, and took a little knife, and cut off a lock of her hair, and gave it to her daughter, and said: "Take care of it, dear child; it is a charm that may be of use to you." Then they took sorrowful leave of each other, and the Princess set off on her journey. As they were riding along by the side of a brook, she felt very thirsty, and said to her maid: "Pray get down and fetch me some water in my golden cup."

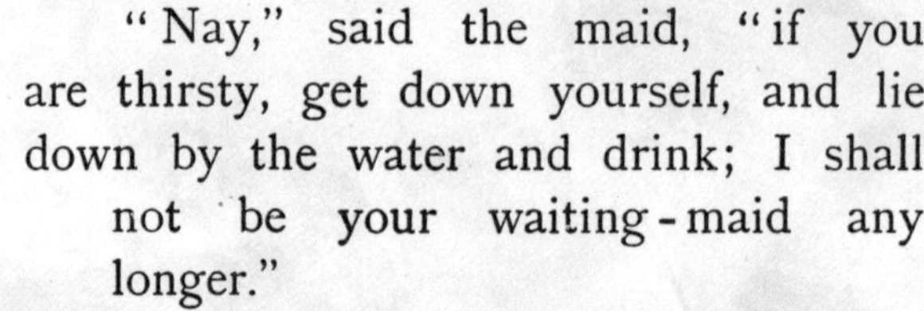

"Nay," said the maid, "if you are thirsty, get down yourself, and lie down by the water and drink; I shall not be your waiting-maid any longer."

She was so thirsty that she got down, and knelt over the little brook and drank, for she was frightened, and dared not bring out her golden cup; and then she wept, and said: "Alas! what will become of me?" And the lock of hair answered her, and said:

"Alas! alas! if thy mother knew it,
Sadly, sadly her heart would rue it."

The Princess said nothing to her maid's ill behaviour, but got upon her horse again.

They rode farther, till the day grew so warm that the bride began to feel very thirsty again; and at last, when they came to a river, she forgot her maid's rude speech, and said: "Pray get down and fetch me some water to drink in my golden cup."

But the maid answered her even more haughtily than before: "Drink if you will, but I shall not be your waiting-maid." The Princess was so thirsty that she got off her horse and lay down, and held her head over the running stream, and cried, and said: "What will become of me?" And the lock of hair answered her again:

"Alas! alas! if thy mother knew it,
Sadly, sadly her heart would rue it."

And as she leaned down to drink, the lock of hair fell from her bosom and floated away, without her seeing it. But her maid saw it, and was very glad, for she knew the charm, and saw that the poor bride would be in her power, now that she had lost the hair. So when the bride had done, and would have got upon Falada again, the maid said: "I shall ride upon Falada, and you may have my horse instead:" so she was forced to give up her horse, and soon afterwards to take off her royal clothes, and put on her maid's shabby ones.

As they drew near the end of their journey, this treacherous servant threatened to kill her mistress if she ever told anyone what had happened. But Falada saw it all and marked it well. Then the waiting-maid got upon Falada, and the real bride was set upon the other horse, and they went on till at last they came to the royal Court. There was great joy at their coming, and the Prince flew to meet them, and lifted the maid from her horse, thinking she

was the one who was to be his wife. She was led to the royal chamber, but the true Princess was told to stay in the court below.

The old King happened to be looking out of the window, and saw her; and as she looked very pretty, and too delicate for a waiting-maid, he went into the royal chamber to ask the bride who it was she had brought with her, that was left standing in the court below. "I brought her with me for the sake of her company on the road," said she; "pray give the girl some work to do, that she may not be idle."

The old King could not for some time think of any work for her; but at last he said: "I have a lad who takes care of my geese; she may go and help him." Now the name of this lad, that the real bride was to help, was Curdken.

Soon after, the false bride said to the Prince: "Dear husband, pray do me one piece of kindness."

"That I will," said the Prince. "Then tell one of your slaughterers to cut off the head of the horse I rode upon, for it was very unruly, and plagued me sadly on the road:" but the truth was, she was much afraid lest Falada should tell all she had done to the Princess. She carried her point, and the faithful Falada was killed; but when the true Princess heard of it she wept, and begged the man to nail up Falada's head against a large dark gate in the city, through which she had to pass every morning and evening, that there she might still see him sometimes. Then the slaughterer said he would do as she wished, cut off the head, and nailed it under the dark gate.

Early the next morning, as she and Curdken went through the gate, she said sorrowfully:

**"Falada, Falada, there thou art hanging!"**

and the head answered:

"Bride, bride, there thou art ganging!
Alas! alas! if thy mother knew it,
Sadly, sadly her heart would rue it."

Then they drove the geese on. And when she came to the meadow, she sat down upon a bank, and let down her waving locks of hair, which were all

of pure silver. And when Curdken saw it glitter in the sun, he ran up, and would have pulled some of the locks out; but she cried:

"Blow, breezes, blow!
Let Curdken's hat go!
Blow, breezes, blow!
Let him after it go!
O'er hills, dales, and rocks,
Away be it whirl'd,
Till the silvery locks
Are all comb'd and curl'd!"

Then there came a wind, that blew off Curdken's hat; and away it flew, and he after it; till, by the time he came back, she had done combing and curling her hair, and put it up again. Then he was angry and sulky, and would not speak to her; but they watched the geese until evening, and then drove them homewards.

The next morning, as they were going through the dark gate, the poor girl looked up at Falada's head, and cried:

"Falada, Falada, there thou art hanging!"

and it answered:

"Bride, bride, there thou art ganging!
Alas! alas! if thy mother knew it,
Sadly, sadly her heart would rue it."

Then she drove on the geese, and sat down again in the meadow, and began to comb out her hair as before; and Curdken ran up to her, and wanted to take hold of it; but she cried quickly:

"Blow, breezes, blow!
Let Curdken's hat go!
Blow, breezes, blow!
Let him after it go!
O'er hills, dales, and rocks,
Away be it whirl'd,
Till the silvery locks
Are all comb'd and curl'd!"

Then the wind came and blew his hat far away, so that he had to run after it; and when he came back, she had done up her hair, and all was safe.

# THE GOOSE GIRL

After they came home, Curdken went to the old King and said: "I cannot have that strange girl to help me to keep the geese any longer."

"Why?" asked the King.

"Because she does nothing but tease me all day long." Then the King made him tell all that had passed.

And Curdken said: "When we go in the morning through the dark gate with our flock of geese, she weeps, and talks with the head of a horse that hangs upon the wall, and says:

"'Falada, Falada, there thou art hanging!"

and the head answers:

"'Bride, bride, there thou art ganging!<br>
Alas! alas! if thy mother knew it,<br>
Sadly, sadly her heart would rue it.'"

And Curdken went on telling what had happened where the geese fed; and how his hat was blown away, and he was forced to run after it, and leave his flock. The old King told him to go out again as usual the next day; and when morning came, he placed himself behind the dark gate, and heard how she spoke to Falada, and how Falada answered; and then he went into the field and hid himself in a bush by the

meadow's side, and saw with his own eyes how they drove the flock of geese, and how, after a little time, she let down her hair that glittered in the sun; and he heard her say:

"Blow, breezes, blow!
Let Curdken's hat go!
Blow, breezes, blow!
Let him after it go!
O'er hills, dales, and rocks,
Away be it whirl'd,
Till the silvery locks
Are all comb'd and curl'd!"

Soon came a gale of wind, and carried away Curdken's hat, while the girl went on combing and curling her hair. All this the old King saw. So he went home without being seen; and when the goose girl came back in the evening, he called her aside, and asked her why she did so; but she burst into tears, and said: "That I must not tell you or any man, or I shall lose my life."

But the old King begged so hard, that she had no peace till she had told him all; and it was lucky for her that she did, for the King ordered royal clothes to be put upon her, and gazed on her with wonder, she was so beautiful. Then he called his son, and told him that he had only the false bride, for that she was merely a waiting-maid, while the true one stood by. And the young King rejoiced when he saw her beauty, and heard how meek and patient she had been; and, without saying anything, ordered a great feast to be got ready for all his Court. The bridegroom sat at the top, with the false Princess on one side, and the true one on the other; but nobody knew her, for she was quite dazzling to their eyes, and was not at all like the little goose girl, now that she had her brilliant dress.

When they had eaten and drank, and were very merry, the old King told all the story, as one that he had once heard of, and asked the true waiting-maid what she thought ought to be done to anyone who would behave thus. "Nothing better," said this false bride, "than that she should be thrown into a cask stuck round with sharp nails, and that two white horses should be put to it, and should drag it from street to street till she is dead." "Thou art she!" said the old King; "and since thou hast judged thyself, it shall be so done to thee." And the young King was married to his true wife, and they reigned over the kingdom in peace and happiness all their lives.

# Goldmaria and Goldfeather

NCE a nobleman had a beautiful daughter named Goldmaria. Her parents one day went on an excursion, and Goldmaria remained at home. On their return, they lost their way in a vast forest, when they were met by a large poodle. "I will lead you into the right path," said the poodle, "if you will give me that which first meets you from your house."

The parents instantly thought of their dear Goldmaria, and feared that she might be the first to meet them; but as the weather became worse, and they had lost their way, they at last consented, and promised the poodle what he required, thinking that the housedog might probably be the first to come to their carriage. They soon reached home; but the first that came to their carriage was Goldmaria. Said the poodle: "She now belongs to me and not to you." The parents besought him to take everything else, only to leave their dear Goldmaria; but the poodle would not hear them and would have Goldmaria, and no prayers were of any avail. A respite of three days would he grant them, and then fetch her away.

Goldmaria employed her time in taking leave of her friends. Amid their tears she was calm and content. On the last evening she said to her mother: "I will now bid farewell to our old neighbour." When she came, the old woman said: "Fear nothing, my child; if thou wilt sleep with me to-night, I will teach thee *to wish*, and that will be highly useful to thee." Goldmaria was quite rejoiced, and went back to her mother to tell her she would pass the night with her neighbour. When Goldmaria rose on the following morning she could conjure forth anything that she *wished*; and, having thanked the old woman, took leave, hoping that, by means of her art, she might be able to see her parents as often as she desired.

When she returned home, the poodle was already there to fetch her away. Goldmaria bade farewell to her disconsolate parents, but made no mention of her having learned *to wish.* On coming to the open country the poodle said to her: "Set thyself on my back, and I will soon bring thee to our journey's end." Goldmaria did so, and in a short time they came to a house, in which were two young maidens. When they entered, the poodle immediately transformed himself into an old woman, the mother of the two maidens.

"Now," said she, "I have three lasses in whom I can find pleasure. Thou, Goldmaria, will be very happy with me, if thou wilt be obedient."

Goldmaria promised to be so, and whenever the old woman said: "Goldmaria, do this, or do that," she would always do it quickly, as she had only to *wish* it.

One day when the old woman, in the likeness of a poodle, went into the forest, she met a comely young man, who had lost his way and was named Goldfeather. The poodle said: "I will conduct thee out of the forest, if thou wilt promise to return and abide with me." Goldfeather answered that he could make no promise, for that he was a king's son, and must speak with his father. At length, however, when he found himself quite unable to recover his path, he was obliged to say *yes*, and promise to belong to the poodle, who then conducted him out of the forest to his father's Court. But at the expiration of three days he returned to fetch away Goldfeather. The father at first would not deliver him up, but was at length forced to comply, when the poodle said: "Goldfeather has himself promised, and he must keep his word." So Goldfeather came to the place where Goldmaria was.

Goldmaria said to Goldfeather: "Be on thy guard against the old woman, for she is a bad one, and can do more than eat bread. To-morrow thou wilt certainly have to mow the grass."

"But," answered Goldfeather, "I cannot; I don't know how I am to do it."

And so it proved; for in the evening the old woman said to him: "Goldfeather, thou must get a scythe ready, for to-morrow thou shalt mow the grass."

Goldfeather then went to Goldmaria and said: "I am to get a scythe ready, and don't know how."

"Oh," said she, "just knock a little on the scythe, then it will soon be ready!" Goldfeather did so, and the scythe was instantly fit for use.

On the following morning the old woman said: "Goldfeather, go and mow the grass." He went first to Goldmaria,

"THEY MET A LARGE POODLE"

and asked her: "How am I to do it? I know nothing of the matter."

Goldmaria answered: "Only strike the scythe, so that it rings, about the time when the old woman brings thee food."

Goldfeather then went to the meadow and laid himself down to sleep; but at the time when his food was to be brought, he struck the scythe so that it rang, and in one

moment all the grass fell down at once. Now came the old woman, who, seeing that all was done, praised him, and promised that he should be rewarded.

On the day following, the old woman said to Goldfeather: "My son, go to-day and sharpen an axe, for thou shalt cut wood." He did not know how to sharpen an axe, and so went to Goldmaria for her instruction. She said: "Take a stone and rub it twice or thrice up and down the axe, and it will instantly be sharp." Goldfeather did so.

Shortly after, the old woman said to him: "Now go into

the forest and hew wood." He went, but could accomplish nothing.

At length came Goldmaria and brought him his breakfast. "Ah," said he, "thou must help me again, for I know nothing about woodcutting!"

"So," answered she, "it seems, then, that I am always to help thee and thou never helpest me."

"Oh, dearest Goldmaria," answered Goldfeather, "I will ever love thee and never forsake thee as long as there is a drop of warm blood within me! Help me but this time out of difficulty."

"Well then," said she, "only turn the axe round and strike the tree." He did so, and in a moment all the wood was hewed. The old mother was astonished at his diligence, and promised that it should be for his advantage. When Goldfeather returned home in the evening, he threw himself on his bed, thought much on his parents, but much more on Goldmaria.

The next day the old woman said: "Thou must get some rakes ready, for to-day, thou shalt all turn the hay and carry it in."

"Mother," said the daughters, "how can we carry in the hay? It is not possible."

"It shall be done, and you must do it," answered the mother. Goldfeather then went, and, with the aid of Goldmaria, prepared the rakes. When both the daughters, together with Goldfeather, were out in the field, where they were joined by Goldmaria, Goldfeather said to her: "How are we to carry in the hay?"

"Just do as I do," answered she; "only lay a stick on the nape of thy neck, and the hay will be soon got in." So when the two daughters were foremost with a small quantity of hay, Goldmaria and Goldfeather placed sticks on the nape of their necks, and all the hay came after them, and they soon had it all together in the place where it was to lie.

On the following day, he was ordered to bring wood home. But when he went for the purpose, he could bring only a very small quantity and was soon weary, so was obliged again to have recourse to Goldmaria, who said to him: "Do as thou didst with the hay;" and when Goldfeather had so done, all the wood was soon in the house Then said the old woman: "Now get some spades in readiness, for to-morrow thou shalt dig clay. Make also some moulds, for thou shalt also make bricks." Now must Goldmaria again give her aid, so that the spades and moulds were soon ready, and when Goldfeather set about digging clay, and could extract none, Goldmaria again came to his assistance, and told him he had only to thrust vigorously with the spade, and there would fly out clay enough. When Goldfeather had finished his task the eldest daughter came and praised him to the skies; whereupon Goldmaria said: "You praise him too much, for I have shared in the work." But the daughter still thought that Goldfeather deserved the greatest praise.

"It bodes no good to me," said Goldmaria to Goldfeather, when the daughter had left them, "that she praised thee so warmly."

But Goldfeather answered: "I will surely be true to thee, dear Goldmaria, as long as I live."

When the old woman came, she ordered the bricks to be made. Goldfeather made them, and, when they were dry,

would carry them to the house, but found them too heavy; recourse must again be had to Goldmaria. "Thou art truly a dolt," said she. "How often have I told thee that thou hadst only to take a stick and lay it on thy neck, and that then all would be easy."

Goldfeather then laid a stick across the nape of his neck, and all the bricks followed him. The old woman next asked him: "Dost thou know how to build an oven?"

"No," answered he, "but I will do my best."

So Goldfeather set to work, but could neither prepare the mortar nor lay the bricks, and must therefore again apply to Goldmaria to help him out of his trouble.

"Oh, thou canst do nothing!" said she. "Take a stick and beat the mortar with it, then it will be fit for use; and for the walls thou canst hammer a bit on a brick, and the oven will be ready." When he had finished, Goldmaria came to him and said: "We must now prepare for travelling; for I heard the old woman say we were too clever, and that when the oven was ready, we should be baked in it. Now I tell thee, Goldfeather, that, if thy life is dear to thee, thou must not leave me; for thou alone canst effect nothing against the old beldam. To-morrow she will allow thee to rest, and will bake thee the day after; be therefore on thy guard." Goldfeather was greatly alarmed, and it proved exactly as Goldmaria had said.

"To-morrow," said the old woman to him, "thou canst rest."

But quite early, just at the break of day, Goldmaria rose and waked Goldfeather. They soon made themselves ready, and when about to set out Goldmaria spat on each side of her chamber door and said: "When the old woman calls me the first time, do thou answer, *I am coming*; and if she calls a second time, answer, *I am coming directly*." In the morning the old woman screamed out for Goldmaria, and the door answered her: "I am coming." When she called a second time, the door answered: "I am coming directly." But no one came.

The old woman at length rose, looked into the chamber and into the kitchen, but no one was in either place. She then waked both her daughters, and said: "Rise up quickly;

Goldmaria and Goldfeather are away, and you must go after them. Go thou first," said she to the younger. "On the declivity of the Blue Mountain there stands a rosebush with a withered rose; that thou must on no account fail to pluck and bring to me." The daughter went in all haste after the fugitives, who had already proceeded a considerable distance, when Goldmaria said to Goldfeather: "Tread on my left foot, and look over my right shoulder whether anyone is coming."

Goldfeather did so and said: "The younger daughter is coming in all haste after us."

Goldmaria thereupon said: "I will then turn myself into a rosebush, and thee into a withered rose; but let not thyself be plucked, and prick her smartly; for if she plucks thee, we are both lost."

When the girl came to the rose, she was about to pluck it, but it pricked her so severely that she was forced to desist. She then returned home and was well scolded for her stupidity.

The old woman then said to the elder daughter: "Do thou now go, and when thou art over the Blue Mountain, thou wilt see a white church, in which there is a preacher in the pulpit: take him by the hand and bring him with thee."

Goldmaria and Goldfeather had in

the meanwhile proceeded farther; but Goldmaria soon said: "Tread on my left foot, and look over my right shoulder whether anyone is coming."

"Yes," answered Goldfeather, "the elder daughter is coming."

"Then," said Goldmaria, "I will turn myself into a church, and thee into a priest; but let her not lay hold of thee, else we are lost."

Now came the daughter and entered the church, but was unable to ascend the pulpit and obliged to return home. At seeing her the old woman's rage exceeded all bounds, and she ran forth herself. Then said Goldmaria to Goldfeather: "Tread on my left foot, and look over my right shoulder whether anyone is coming after us."

"Yes," answered Goldfeather, "the old woman herself is now coming."

"Then I will turn myself into a pond, and thee into a duck; but I beseech thee, Goldfeather, let not thyself be enticed to the edge, so that she may take hold of thee; but take the gold rings, which she will cast in for the purpose of catching thee, if thou canst get them without danger."

Now came the old woman to the pond, and would decoy the duck, which continued swimming about. She threw in her gold rings, one after another, but the duck was not to be so tempted; and when she had thrown in the last she was so angry that she resolved to drink up the pond, and, laying herself down for the purpose, drank so long that she burst. Goldmaria and Goldfeather now resumed their natural forms, and swore eternal fidelity to each other, and that they would never part. From the old woman there was now nothing more to fear.

They at length reached the city in which Goldfeather's father resided. When they came before the palace, and Goldfeather was about to enter, Goldmaria said to him: "Hear me, Goldfeather; I have only one request to make thee, that thou mayest not forget me when thou art in thy father's house, and leave me here without, standing on the broad stone. Beware that no one kisses thee; for then thou wilt instantly forget me." Goldfeather promised, and recollected the warning on entering the house; and when his father and mother hastened to welcome him, he did not kiss them. But when he entered an apartment, there sat his old betrothed, whose name was Menne, who, the instant she saw him, sprang up for joy and kissed him. In one moment all remembrance of Goldmaria was banished from his mind. She stood long without, expecting that he would send for her; but, finding that no one came, she wept for a long time, then took her departure, hired a neat little cottage opposite the palace, and gave herself out as a seamstress. Being admirably skilled in needlework, she soon got an abundance of work; no young person in the city being able to sew more curiously and beautifully.

The young sparks of the Court had in the meantime discovered what a handsome maiden Goldmaria was. But Goldmaria paid no heed to them, and never looked from her work, when they passed before her window. Among these young courtiers there were three brothers, all of whom were deeply in love with Goldmaria. They one day begged some fine linen of their mother, saying that Goldmaria worked so delicately, they wished her to make them some collars. The eldest was the first that went to Goldmaria, wished her a good day, and sat down to converse with her. "To-morrow evening you can fetch your collars," said Goldmaria. When the time came for fetching the collars, she invited him to stay awhile, and he remained till bedtime. When he was about to take leave, she said to him that he was welcome to stay there that night, which the young man was perfectly ready to do. When Goldmaria was retiring to rest, she requested him to go and lock the door of the house, and when he touched the lock, she cried out:

> "Man to lock and lock to man,
> Then go to rest I calmly can."

There he was obliged to remain the whole night. In the morning, when Goldmaria rose, she recollected that he was yet there, and said:

> "Man from lock and lock from man,
> Then give thanks for his sleep he can."

He then entered, returned thanks for his tranquil sleep, took his collars, with which he was much pleased, and went away. At home he made no mention of his

adventure. His younger brother then said: "This evening I must away to the seamstress."

He went accordingly, and said: "I wish to have some collars made like my brother's."

"Those you can easily have," said Goldmaria; "sit down and stay a little."

They then entered into conversation, while Goldmaria sewed. When it was time for him to depart, she told him that he was welcome to stay there that night; but before she withdrew, she said: "I have quite forgotten to fasten the garden door; would you have the kindness to fasten it for me?"

"Most willingly," answered he, and hastened away for the purpose; but the instant he touched the ring of the door, she cried out:

"Man to ring and ring to man,
Then go to rest I calmly can."

He was unable to get loose, and had to remain standing until morning, when Goldmaria rose and said:

"Man from ring and ring from man,
Then give thanks for his sleep he can."

Being released, he entered and thanked her for his comfortable sleep.

On his return home with the collars, his elder brother instantly asked him where he had been standing all night.

"What?" answered he. "Why, I have been sleeping."

"That's not true," said the other; "so tell me where thou

hast been standing, and I'll tell thee where I was standing."

He then said: "I have been standing by the garden door."

"And I by the house door," said the other. They then agreed not to say a word of what had befallen them to their youngest brother, that he might also be tricked.

In the evening the youngest brother went. "Good evening, Goldmaria," said he; "wilt thou make me two or three collars like those of my brothers?"

"Most willingly," answered Goldmaria; "just sit down a little while and stay."

When evening was over, she also requested him to remain there all night; but just as she was about to retire, she said to him: "Oh, my calf is not yet tethered, and is running about the yard! Do me the kindness——"

"With pleasure," answered he, running out; but on his touching the rope, she cried:

"Man to rope and rope to man,
Then go to rest I calmly can."

The calf then began running with him, over stock and stone, and through thick and thin, the whole night long. In the morning Goldmaria recollected that the young man was still running about with the calf, and said:

"Man from rope and rope from man,
Then give thanks for his sleep he can."

He then entered, thanked her for his comfortable sleep, and was exceedingly delighted with his collars, which were much handsomer than those she had made for his brothers. On his return home, and his brothers asking him how he had passed the night, he would not confess that he had been running about with the calf.

Matters had in the meantime proceeded so far with Goldfeather and Menne, that the day was fixed for their marriage. When the carriage with the bridal pair came down from the palace, and was passing by Goldmaria's window, she *wished* that it might sink in a deep swamp that was exactly before her door. The carriage stuck fast accordingly, so that neither horses nor men could draw it from the spot. At this the old King was sorely vexed, and ordered more horses to be put to, and that more men should assist, but all to no purpose. Among the retinue, which attended the bridegroom to church, were the three brothers before-mentioned, the eldest of whom said to the King: "Sir King, here in this small house there dwells a maiden that can *wish* whatever she desires; and she has surely wished the carriage to stick fast in this place."

"How dost thou know that she can do so?" asked the old King.

The young man answered:

"She lately wished me to the house door, and there I was obliged to stand all night."

"Yes," said the second brother, "but when she has wished anyone fast, she can also wish him loose."

"And how dost thou know that?" enquired the King.

"I was lately obliged to stand the whole night at her garden door; but in the morning she released me."

The old King would then instantly send to Goldmaria, but the youngest brother said:

"Sir King, the young woman has also a calf that has the strength of ten horses. Let the bridegroom go to her and beg her to lend us the calf; the carriage will then be soon set free."

"That I'll do most readily," said the bridegroom, at the same time alighting from the vehicle and going to Goldmaria, whom he besought to lend him her calf, which, as he had heard, possessed such wonderful power.

"The calf you can have and welcome," answered she, "but you must first promise that I shall be invited to the wedding, together with my doves."

This the bridegroom promised, and as soon as the calf was harnessed to the vehicle, it drew it forth with perfect ease.

After the ceremony, when the young couple had returned home, and many guests were assembled, Goldmaria also made her appearance with her two doves. She met with a friendly reception, and was conducted into the saloon, having a dove perched on each shoulder. At table the most costly dishes were served up, portions of which were set before Goldmaria; but she touched nothing, and sat sad and silent. At seeing so fair a damsel sitting so sad, and tasting nothing, the guests were astonished, and on asking her the cause, the doves answered:

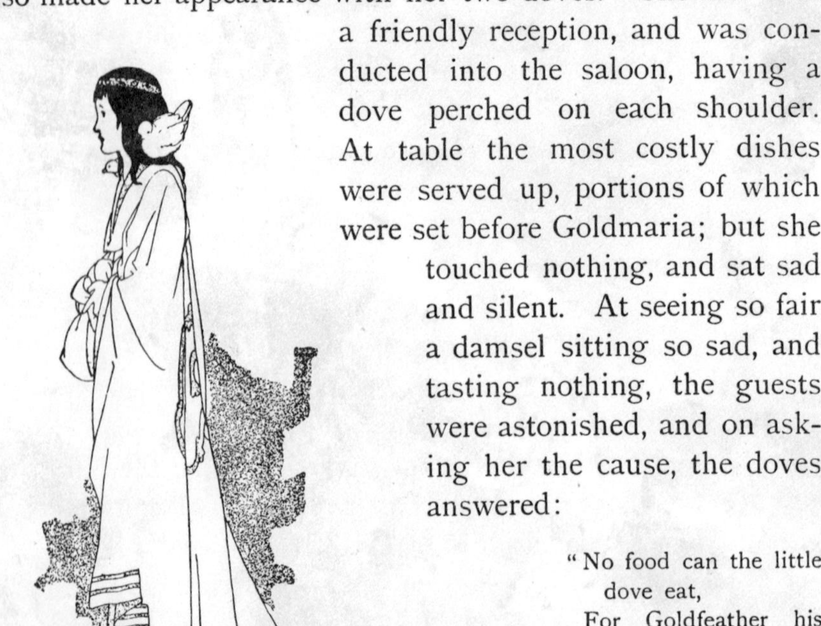

"No food can the little dove eat,
For Goldfeather his bride has forgotten,
And left on the stone in the street."

The bridegroom, hearing this, ordered the servants to place before her viands yet more costly; but Goldmaria touched nothing, and the doves repeated:

> "No food can the little dove eat,
> For Goldfeather his bride has forgotten,
> And left on the stone in the street."

At this the bridegroom became lost in thought, looked steadfastly at Goldmaria, and recognized her. He then addressed his bride: "My dear bride, I pray thee answer me one question. I have a cabinet in which there are two keys, an old one, which I once lost, but have now found again, and a new one, which I procured in place of the old one, when that was lost. Tell me now which of the two I ought to use first, the old one or the new?"

She answered: "Thou shouldst first use the old one."

"Thou hast now," replied he, "pronounced thy own sentence; for this is my dear Goldmaria, with whom I have shared joy and sorrow at the old witch's in the forest, who at all times aided me, who saved me, and to whom I have sworn eternal fidelity."

Menne then, having no alternative, renounced Goldfeather, and all the people, and his and her parents, declared there was no one that so well deserved to be his wife as Goldmaria. They were then married and lived happily together for very many years

# Hop o' my Thumb

ONCE upon a time there was a poor woodman who had seven children, all boys, the eldest no more than ten, the youngest only seven. This youngest was a puny little chap who rarely spoke a word; he was indeed the smallest person ever seen, being when born no bigger than a thumb, and thus he got the name of Hop o' my Thumb. Still he was by far cleverer than any of his brothers, and though he spoke but little he heard more than was imagined. The woodman and his wife at length became so poor that they could no longer give their children their usual food. One evening when the boys were in bed, the husband, sighing deeply, said:

"You see, dear wife, it is impossible for us to maintain our children any longer, and to see them die of hunger before my eyes is what I never could support. I am determined to take them to-morrow morning to the forest, and leave them in the thickest part of it, so that it will be impossible to find their way back."

"Ah!" cried the poor wife, "you cannot consent to be the death of your own children!" but at length, considering how dreadful it would be to see them die of hunger before her eyes, she consented to her husband's proposal, and went sobbing to bed.

Hop o' my Thumb had been all the time awake; and hearing his father talk more earnestly than usual, slipped away from his brothers, and crept under his father's bed to hear all that might be said without being seen. When his father and mother left off talking, he got back to his own place, and passed the night thinking what he should do. He rose early and ran to the river's side, filled his pockets with white pebbles, and returned home.

All set out, as their father and mother had agreed, and Hop o' my Thumb said not a word of what he had discovered. They reached a forest that was so thick, that at ten paces distant they could not see each other. The woodman set to work, cutting down wood, and the children began to gather all the twigs, and to make faggots of them. Then the father and mother, observing them all busy, slipped away without being perceived, and getting into a by-path, soon lost sight of the forest.

In a short time the children, finding themselves alone, began to cry as loud as they could. Hop o' my Thumb let them cry; for he knew how to conduct them safely home, having taken care to drop the white pebbles he had in his pocket the whole of the way by which they had come: he therefore only said:

"Never mind, my lads: father and mother have left us by ourselves; only take care to follow me, and I will lead you back again."

They followed Hop o' my Thumb, who soon brought them to their father's house, by the very same path by which they had come. Just as the woodman and his wife had returned home without their children, a gentleman of the village had sent to pay them two guineas, which had so long been owing for work they had done, that they never expected to receive it; this money quite rejoiced their hearts; for the poor creatures were exceedingly hungry, and had nc means of getting anything to eat. The woodman sent his wife out to buy some meat; and as it was a long time since she had made a hearty meal, she bought enough for six or eight persons: but it might be that she had not yet learned to leave out her children, when she was thinking of what would be enough for dinner. She and her husband had no sooner eaten heartily than she cried out:

"Alas! where are our poor children? How they would feast on what we have left! It was all your fault. I told you over and over that we should repent the hour when we

left them to starve in the forest! Oh, mercy! they may perhaps be already eaten up by the wolves!"

The woodman grew angry with his wife, who repeated more than twenty times, that he would repent of what he had done, and that she had again and again told him so: he at last threatened to give her a good beating if she did not hold her tongue: not but that he was quite as sorry as his wife for what had happened, but that her scolding teased him.

"Alas!" repeated she, "what is become of my dear children?" and once she said this so loud that the children, who were listening at the door, cried out together:

"Here we are, mother, here we are!"

She flew to let them in, and kissed every one of them.

"How glad I am to see you, you little rogues!" said she. "Are you not tired and hungry? Ah, poor little Bobby! why, thou art dirt all over, my child! come hither, and let me wash thy face."

Bobby was the youngest excepting Hop o' my Thumb; and had always been his mother's favourite. The children sat down to dinner, and ate quite heartily. The parents were quite delighted at having their children again, and this continued till their money was all spent: then, finding themselves in the same condition as before, they, by degrees, again determined to leave them once more in the forest; and that they might not a second time be disappointed, they resolved to lead them a much greater distance than at first. They could not, however, consult with each other on this business so secretly but Hop o' my Thumb found means to overhear all that passed. It gave him no uneasiness, for he thought nothing could be easier than to do exactly the same as he had done before: but though he rose early to go to the river's side and get the pebbles, he could not get out, for the door was locked. Hop o' my Thumb was at a loss what to do; but his mother having given each of the children a piece of bread for breakfast, he thought he could make his share serve the same purpose as the pebbles. He accordingly put it carefully into his pocket.

It was not long before they set out, and their parents took care to lead them into the very thickest and darkest part of the forest, and then slipped away along a by-path as before. This did not give Hop o' my Thumb any concern, for he thought himself quite sure of getting back by means of the crumbs he had strewed by the way; but what was his surprise at finding that not a morsel was left! The birds had eaten it all up!

The poor children were in a terrible plight; for the further they went, the more they found it difficult to get out of the forest. At length night came on, and they mistook the whistling of the wind for the howling of wolves, and every moment expected to be devoured.

When it began to grow light, Hop o' my Thumb climbed to the top of a tree, and looked on all sides, to discover, if possible, some means of assistance: he saw a small light like that of a candle, but it was at a great distance beyond the forest: he came down thinking to find his way to it, but it had disappeared; and he was in perplexity what to do next. They continued walking in the direction in which he had seen the light, and at last, having reached the end of the forest, again got sight of it. They quickened their steps, and after great fatigue arrived at the house in which it was. They knocked at the door, which was opened by a good-natured-looking lady, who asked what brought them thither? Hop o' my Thumb answered, that they were poor children who had lost their way in the forest, and begged that she would give them a bed till morning.

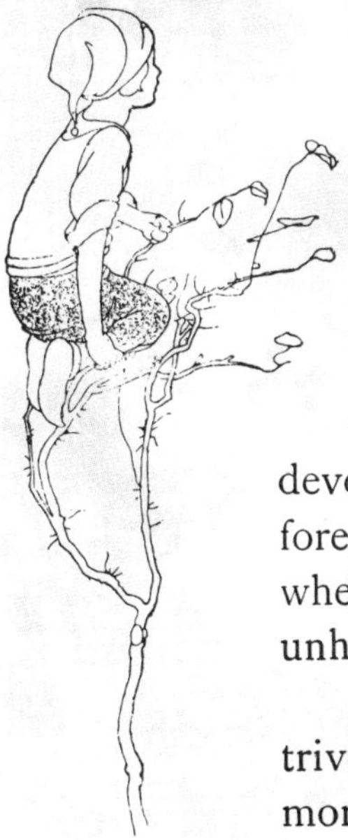

The lady, seeing they had such pretty faces, began to shed tears, and said:

"Ah! poor children, whither are you come? Do you not know that this is the house of an Ogre who eats little boys and girls?"

"Alas!" replied Hop o' my Thumb, "what shall we do? If we go back to the forest, it is certain that we shall be devoured by the wolves; we had rather, therefore, be eaten up by the gentleman; besides, when he sees us, he may perhaps pity our unhappy condition, and spare our lives."

The Ogre's wife, thinking she could contrive to hide them from her husband till the morning, let them in, and made them warm

themselves by a good fire, before which there was a whole sheep roasting for the Ogre's supper. When they had stood a short time by the fire, there came a loud knocking at the door. It was the Ogre! His wife hurried the children under the bed, telling them to lie still: she then let her husband in.

The Ogre immediately asked if the supper was ready, and if the wine was fetched from the cellar, and then sat down to table. Presently he began to sniff right and left, saying he smelled child's flesh.

"It must be this calf which has just been killed," answered his wife.

"I smell child's flesh," cried the Ogre. "I smell child's flesh; there is something going on I do not understand."

Saying this, he rose and went straight to the bed.

"Ah! ah! deceitful creature, is it thus you think to cheat me? Wretch! but that thou art old and tough, I would eat thee too! But come, what thou hast done is lucky enough, for the brats will make a nice dish for three ogres, my particular friends, who are to dine with me to-morrow."

He drew them out one by one from under the bed. The

poor children fell on their knees, begging his pardon as well as they could speak; but this Ogre was one of the cruellest of all the Ogres, and, far from feeling any pity, began to devour them already with his eyes, and told his wife "they would be delicious morsels if she served them up with a savoury sauce". He then fetched a large knife, and began to sharpen it on a long whetstone which he held in his left hand, approaching all the time nearer and nearer to the bed. The Ogre took up one of the children, and was going to set about cutting him to pieces, when his wife said to him:

"What in the world makes you take the trouble of killing them to-night? Will it not be time enough to-morrow morning?"

"Hold your prating," replied the Ogre, "they will be the tenderer for keeping."

"But you have so much meat in the house already," answered his wife; "here is a calf, two sheep, and half a pig."

"Right," said the Ogre; "give them a good supper, that they may not lose their plumpness, and send them to bed."

The good creature accordingly gave them a plentiful supper: but the poor children were much too frightened to eat. As for the Ogre, he sat down to his wine delighted with the thought of giving his friends so delicate a repast on the morrow, and, after drinking up all his wine, he at once went to bed.

The Ogre had seven daughters, all very young. They

had fair complexions, because they fed on raw meat like their father; but they had small grey eyes, quite round, and sunk in their heads, hooked noses, wide mouths, and very long sharp teeth standing at a great distance from each other. They were too young to have done a great deal of

mischief; but they gave signs of being, when older, as cruel as their father, for they already delighted in biting young children. These young ogresses had been put to bed early, all in one very large bed, and each had a crown of gold on her head. There was in the same chamber another bed of equal size, and in this the Ogre's wife put the seven little boys.

Hop o' my Thumb, having observed that the Ogresses had all crowns of gold upon their heads, and fearing the Ogre might awake and repent of not having killed him and his brothers, got out of bed about midnight, as softly as he could, and, taking off their nightcaps and his own, crept to the Ogre's daughters, took off their crowns, and put the nightcaps on their heads instead; he then put the crowns on himself and his brothers, and again got into bed.

Everything succeeded well. The Ogre, waking soon after midnight, was sorry he had deferred what he could have done that very night. He therefore hurried out of bed, and, taking up his large knife,—

"Let us see," said he, "what the young rogues are about, and do the job at once!" He stalked quietly to the room in which his daughters slept, and going up to the bed which held the boys, who, excepting Hop o' my Thumb, were all asleep, he felt their heads one by one.

The Ogre, feeling the crowns of gold, said to himself: "I had like to have made a pretty mistake!" He went next to the bed which held his daughters, and feeling the nightcaps: "Ah, here you are, my lads!" said he; and instantly killed all his daughters, one by one. Well satisfied, he returned to bed.

As soon as Hop o' my Thumb heard him snoring, he awoke his brothers, and told them to put on their clothes quickly, and follow him. They stole down softly to the garden, and then jumped from the walls into the road. They ran with all their strength the whole night, but were all the time so terrified they scarcely knew which way to take.

When the Ogre awoke in the morning, he said to his wife: "Prythee, go and dress the young rogues I saw last night."

The Ogress was surprised at her husband's kindness, not dreaming of the real meaning of his words. She went upstairs, and the first thing she beheld was her seven daughters all killed. The Ogre, fearing his wife might spend too much time in what he had set her about, went himself to help her, and was not less surprised than she had been at the shocking spectacle.

"Ah! what have I done!" cried he; "but the little varlets shall pay for it, I warrant them!"

He threw some water on his wife's face; and as soon as she recovered he said to her:

"Bring me quickly my seven-league boots, that I may go and catch the little vipers."

The Ogre set out with all speed, and after striding over different parts of the country, at last turned into the very road in which the poor children were journeying towards their father's house, which they had nearly reached. They had seen the Ogre striding from mountain to mountain, and crossing rivers at one step. Hop o' my Thumb perceiving a hollow place under a rock, made his brothers get into it, and then stepped in himself, keeping his eye fixed on the Ogre to see what he would do next.

The Ogre, finding himself tired with the journey he had made,—for seven-league boots are very fatiguing—began to think of resting himself, and happened to sit down on the very rock in which the poor children lay concealed. Being overcome with fatigue he fell asleep, and soon began to snore so terribly that the little fellows were as frightened as when the Ogre stood over them with a knife in his hand, intending to kill them. Hop o' my Thumb, seeing how much his brothers were terrified, said to them:

"Courage, my lads! You have nothing to do but to steal away while the Ogre is fast asleep, and leave me to shift for myself."

The brothers followed his advice, and were very soon at their father's house. In the meantime, Hop o' my Thumb went softly up to the Ogre, and gently pulled off the seven-league boots, and drew them on his own legs; for though the boots were very large, as they were fairies they could make themselves smaller, so as to fit any leg they pleased.

Hop o' my Thumb had no sooner made sure of the Ogre's seven-league boots, than he determined to go to the palace, and offer his services to carry orders from the king to his army, and bring His Majesty the earliest accounts of the battle in which it was at that time engaged.

He had not proceeded many strides before he heard a voice which desired him to stop. Hop o' my Thumb looked about him to discover whence it came, and the same voice continued:

"Listen, Hop o' my Thumb, to what I am about to say. Go not to the palace. Waste no time; the Ogre sleeps; he may awake. Know, Hop o' my Thumb, that the boots you took from the Ogre while asleep are two fairies; I am the eldest of them. We have observed the clever feats you have performed, and have resolved to bestow upon you the gift of riches, if you will once more employ your wits to good purpose, and be as brave as before. But fairies are not allowed to speak such matters as these. Break the shell of the largest nut you can find in your pocket, and in it is a paper which will tell you all that is necessary to be done."

Hop o' my Thumb, instead of wondering what had happened, instantly searched his pocket for the nut, and, having cracked it with his teeth, found in it a piece of paper, which he read as follows:—

"Hie thee to the Ogre's door,
These words speak, and no word more:
Ogress, Ogre cannot come;
Great key give to Hop o' my Thumb."

Hop o' my Thumb began to say the two last lines over and over again, that he might not forget them; and when he thought he had learned them by heart, he made two or three of his largest strides, and reached the Ogre's door. He knocked loudly, and for the second time was received by the Ogre's wife, who at sight of Hop o' my Thumb started back, as if she would have shut the door; but Hop o' my Thumb, knowing he had not a moment to lose, made as if he did not perceive how much she was afflicted at seeing the person who had caused her daughters to be killed by their own father.

Hop o' my Thumb accordingly began to talk as if he was in a great hurry, saying that matters were now changed; that the Ogre, having laid hold of him and his brothers as they were gathering nuts by the side of a hedge, was going to take them back to his house, when all at once the Ogre perceived a number of men who looked like lords, and were on the finest horses ever beheld, coming up to him at full speed; that he soon found they were sent by the king, with a message to borrow of the Ogre a large sum of money, the king believing him to be the richest of his subjects; that the lords finding themselves fatigued with the long journey they had made, the Ogre had desired them to proceed no farther, as he had with him a messenger who would not fail of doing cleverly whatever he was employed about; that the great lords had thanked the Ogre a thousand times, and, in the name of the king, had bestowed upon him the honourable title of Duke of Draggletail; that the Ogre had then taken off his boots, and helped to draw them on Hop o' my Thumb's legs, and charging him to make haste, gave him the following message:—

"Ogress, Ogre cannot come;
Great key give to Hop o' my Thumb."

The Ogress, seeing her husband's boots, and being mightily delighted with the thoughts of becoming Duchess of Draggletail, and living at Court, was ready to believe all that was told her. She

fetched the great key and gave it to Hop o' my Thumb, telling him where to find the chest of money and jewels to which it belonged. Hop o' my Thumb took as much of these treasures as he thought would be sufficient to maintain his father, mother, and brothers without the fatigue of hard labour, saying to himself all the time, that it was better that an honest woodm[illegible] should have a small n[illegible]h vast riches, than [illegible] should make no use o[illegible]

In [illegible] o' my Thumb returned [illegible]fully received by the w[illegible] fame of his boots havi[illegible] at Court, the king se[illegible]t is said, employed hi[illegible]mportant affairs of his [illegible] that he became one of the richest of his subj[illegible]

As for the Ogre, he fell in his sleep from the corner of the rock, from which Hop o' my Thumb and his brothers had escaped, to the ground, and bruised himself so much that he could not stir; he therefore stretched himself out at full length, and waited for someone to come and assist him. But though several woodmen, passing near the place, and hearing the Ogre groan, went up to ask him what was the matter, yet the Ogre was so exceedingly big, that they could not have carried even one of his legs; so they were obliged to leave him; till at length the night came on, when a large serpent came out of a neighbouring wood, and stung him so that he died miserably.

As soon as Hop o' my Thumb, who was become the king's favourite, heard the news of the Ogre's death, he informed His Majesty of all that the good-natured Ogress had done to save the lives of him and his brothers. The king was so pleased that he asked Hop o' my Thumb if there was any favour he could bestow upon her.

Hop o' my Thumb thanked the king, and desired that the Ogress might obtain the honourable title of Duchess of Draggletail; which was no sooner asked than granted. The Ogress came to Court and lived happily for many years, enjoying the vast fortune she found in the Ogre's coffers.

As for Hop o' my Thumb, he every day grew more witty and brave; till at last the king made him the greatest lord in the kingdom, and put all affairs under his direction.

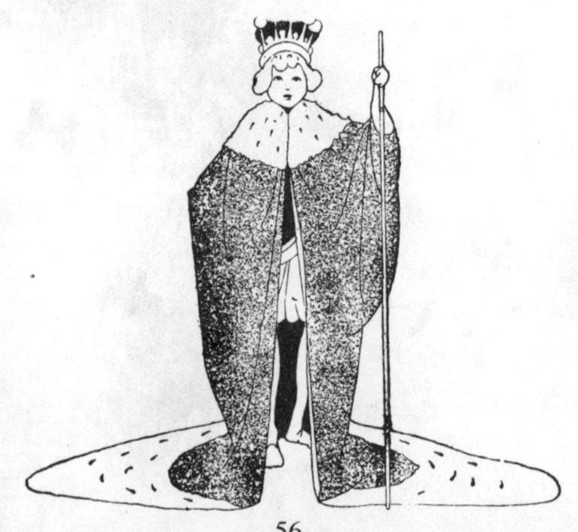

# The Little Tin Soldier

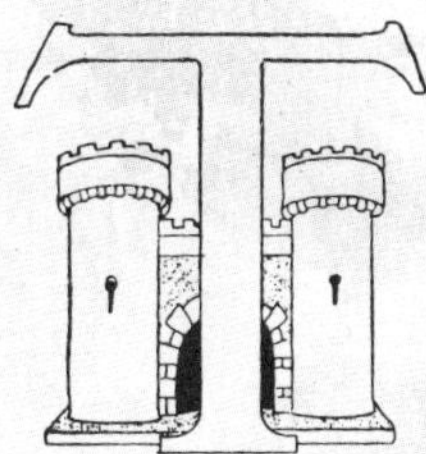

THE soldiers were like each other to a hair—all but one, who had only one leg, because he had been made last, when there was not quite enough tin left; and it is this one-legged tin soldier's fortunes that seem worthy of being told.

On the table where they stood were other playthings, but the most charming of all was a pretty pasteboard castle. Through its little windows one could look into the rooms. In front stood some tiny trees, clustering round a little mirror representing a lake. Some waxen swans swam on the lake and were reflected in it.

All this was very pretty, but prettiest of all was a little lady standing in the doorway of the castle. She, too, was cut out of pasteboard, but she had on a frock of the softest muslin, and a narrow sky-blue riband was flung across her shoulders like a scarf, and in the middle of this scarf was set a glittering tinsel rose. The little lady was a dancer, and she stretched out both her arms, and raised one of her legs so high in the air that the tin soldier could not see it, and thought she had, like himself, only one leg.

"That would be just the wife for me," thought he, "but then she is of too high a rank. She lives in a castle, and I have only a box; and even that is not my own, for five and twenty men live in it. Still, I must make her acquaintance." Then he laid himself down at full length behind a snuff-box, so that he had a full view of the delicate little lady still standing on one leg without losing her balance.

When evening came, all the other tin soldiers were put into the box, and the people of the house went to bed. Then the playthings began to have their own games. The tin soldiers rattled in the box, for they wished to play too, but the lid would not open. The nutcrackers cut capers, and the slate pencil danced on the table. There was such a noise that the canary woke and began to talk too; but he always talked in verse. The only two who did not move from their places were the tin soldier and the dancer. She remained standing on the very tip of her toe, with outstretched arms; and he stood just as firmly on his one leg, never for a moment taking his eyes off her.

Twelve o'clock struck, and with a crash the lid of the snuff-box sprang open—there was no snuff in it, it was only a toy puzzle—and out jumped a little black conjurer. "Tin soldier!" said the conjurer, "please keep your eyes to yourself!"

But the tin soldier pretended not to hear.

"Well, just wait till to-morrow!" said the conjurer.

When the children got up next morning, the tin soldier

was placed on the window ledge, and, whether the conjurer or the wind caused it, all at once the window flew open, and out fell the tin soldier, head foremost, from the third story to the ground. It was a dreadful fall, for he fell headfirst into the street, and at last rested with his cap and bayonet stuck between two paving stones, and his one leg in the air.

The servant-maid and the little boy came downstairs directly to look for him; but though they nearly trod on him, they could not see him. If the tin soldier had but called out, "Here I am!" they might easily have found him; but he thought it would not be becoming to cry out, as he was in uniform.

Presently it began to rain a perfect downpour. When it was over, two little street arabs came by.

"Look!" said one, "there is a tin soldier. Let him have a sail."

So they made a boat out of newspaper, and put the tin soldier into it. Away he sailed down the gutter, both children running along by the side, clapping their hands. The paper boat rocked to and fro, and every now and then was whirled round so quickly that the tin soldier became quite giddy. Still he did not move a muscle, but looked straight before him, and held his musket tightly clasped.

All at once the boat was carried into a long drain, where the tin soldier found it as dark as in his own box.

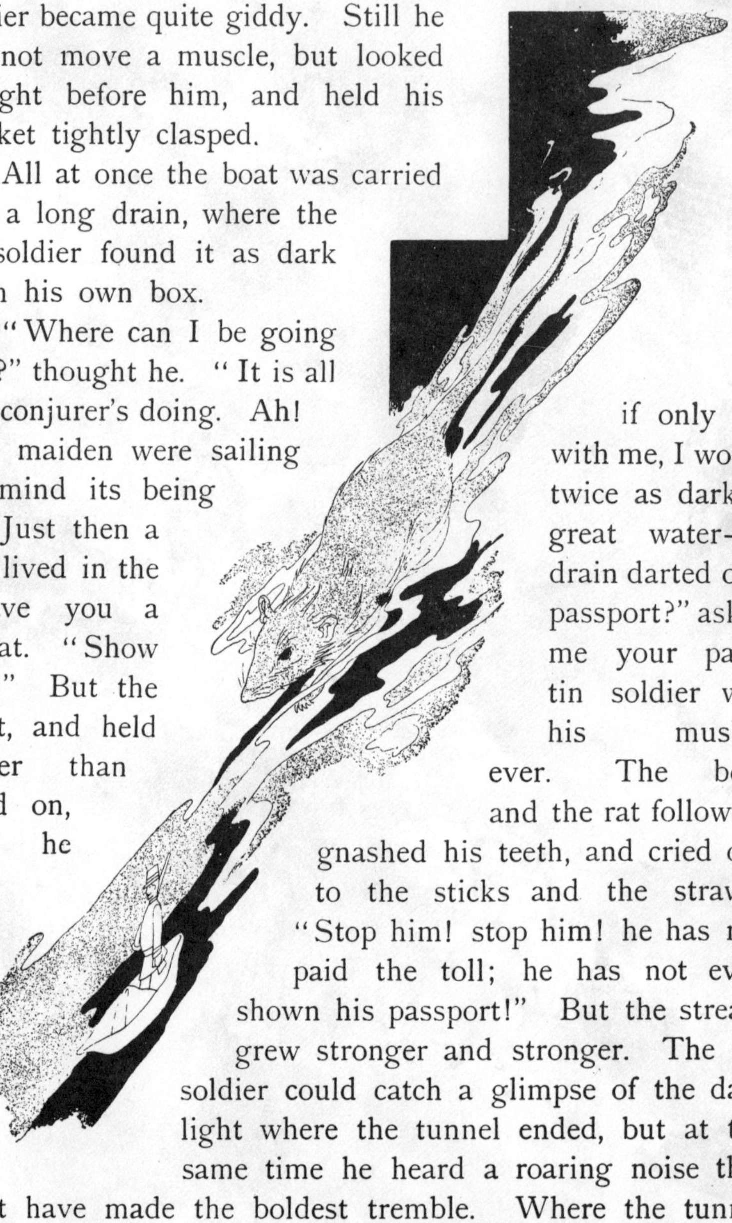

"Where can I be going now?" thought he. "It is all that conjurer's doing. Ah! if only the little maiden were sailing with me, I would not mind its being twice as dark."

Just then a great water-rat that lived in the drain darted out. "Have you a passport?" asked the rat. "Show me your passport!" But the tin soldier was silent, and held his musket tighter than ever. The boat sailed on, and the rat followed. How he gnashed his teeth, and cried out to the sticks and the straws: "Stop him! stop him! he has not paid the toll; he has not even shown his passport!" But the stream grew stronger and stronger. The tin soldier could catch a glimpse of the daylight where the tunnel ended, but at the same time he heard a roaring noise that might have made the boldest tremble. Where the tunnel ended, the water of the gutter fell into a great canal. This was as dangerous for the tin soldier as a waterfall would be for us.

The fall was now so close that he could no longer stand upright. The boat darted forwards; the poor tin soldier held himself as stiffly as possible, so that no one could accuse him of having even blinked. The boat span round three or four times, and was filled with water to the brim; it must sink now!

The tin soldier stood up to his neck in water; but deeper and deeper sank the boat, and softer and softer grew the paper, till the water was over the soldier's head. He thought of the pretty little dancer whom he should never see again, and these words rang in his ears:—

Fare on, thou soldier brave!
Life must end in the grave.

The paper split in two, and the tin soldier fell through the rent, and was at once swallowed by a large fish. Oh, how dark it was! darker even than in the tunnel, and much narrower too. But the tin soldier was as constant as ever, and lay there at full length, still shouldering his arms.

The fish swam to and fro, and made the strangest movements, but at last he became quite still. After a while, a flash of lightning seemed to dart through him, and the daylight shone brightly, and someone cried out: "I declare! here is the tin soldier!" The fish had been caught, taken to the market, sold, and brought into the kitchen, where the servant-girl was cutting him up with a large knife. She seized the tin soldier by the middle with two of her fingers,

and took him into the parlour, where everyone was eager to see the wonderful man who had travelled in a fish.

They set him on the table, and the tin soldier was in the very room in which he had been before. He saw the same children, the same playthings on the table—among them the beautiful castle with the pretty little dancing maiden, still standing upon one leg, while she held the other high in the air; she too was constant. It quite touched the tin soldier. He looked at her, and she looked at him, but neither spoke a word.

And now one of the boys took the soldier and threw him into the stove. He gave no reason for doing so; but no doubt it was the fault of the conjurer in the snuff-box.

The tin soldier now stood in a blaze of light. He felt extremely hot, but whether from the fire, or from the flames of love, he did not know. He had entirely lost his colour. Whether this was the result of his travels, or the effect of strong feeling, I know not. He looked at the little lady, and she looked at him, and he felt that he was melting; but, constant as ever, he still stood shouldering his arms. A door opened, and the draught caught the dancer; and, like a sylph, she flew straightway into the stove to the tin soldier. Instantly she was in a blaze and was gone. The soldier was melted and dripped down among the ashes; and when the maid cleaned out the fireplace the next day, she found his remains in the shape of a little tin heart. Of the dancer, all that was left was the tinsel rose, and that was burnt as black as coal.

THE CONJURER SCOLDS THE LITTLE TIN SOLDIER

# Sindbad the Sailor

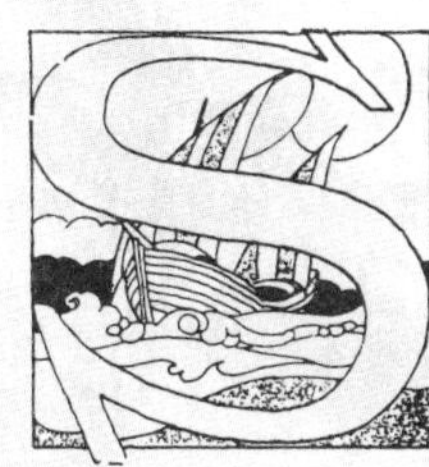

SINDBAD THE SAILOR, after all his adventures and wanderings, settled down in happiness and prosperity in Bagdad. Here are the accounts which he told to his friends of his seven marvellous voyages.

## THE FIRST VOYAGE

My father died while I was young and left me a fortune. Having no one to restrain my conduct, I fell into a state of dissipation, by which I not only wasted my time, but injured my health, and destroyed my property.

When I recovered, I collected together the remains of my fortune, and purchased merchandise, with which I embarked on board a vessel for the port of Balsora.

During the voyage we touched at several islands, where we sold or exchanged our goods. We were one day becalmed near a small island. As its appearance was inviting, we determined to dine upon it. But while we were laughing and preparing for dinner, the island began to move, and at the same moment the people in the ship called out that we were on the back of a monstrous whale. Some jumped into the boat, and others swam to the ship; but before I could get off the animal dived into the sea, and I had only time to catch hold of a piece of wood that had been brought from the ship to serve as a table. Upon this piece of timber I was carried away by the current, the others having reached the vessel; and a gale having sprung up, the ship sailed without me.

I floated during that and the succeeding night, but the following morning was thrown on a small island.

I found fresh water and fruit. I looked about for some place of habitation, but found none. There were a number of colts grazing together, but no traces of other animals. When evening approached I took some more fruit, and climbed into a tree as a resting-place. About midnight the sounds of trumpets and drums seemed to pass around the island, which continued until morning, when again it seemed to be uninhabited. On the next day I found that the island was small, and that no other land was in sight. I therefore gave myself up as lost. Nor were my apprehensions diminished, when I found that the shore abounded with enormous serpents and other sea monsters. I found, however, that they were timid, and that the rattling of sticks would induce them to dive into the water.

I climbed the tree next night, and the drums and trumpets returned as before. On the third day, I had the satisfaction of perceiving a body of men, who, on landing, were astonished to find me there. Having related to them how I came hither, they told me they were grooms of King Mihrage; that the island belonged to genii, who visited it every night with drums and trumpets; that the genii had allowed their sovereign to train his colts upon the island; and that they, being sent every six months to select some, had arrived for that purpose.

The grooms carried me to King Mihrage, who allowed me apartments in his palace.

One day I saw men unloading a ship in the harbour, and perceived that some of the bales were those which I had embarked for Balsora. Going up to the captain, I said:

"Captain, I am Sindbad."

"Surely," said he, "I and the passengers saw Sindbad swallowed in the waves many hundred miles away."

Some others, however, coming up, I was recognized; and the captain then restored me the bales, with many congratulations. I made a valuable present to King Mihrage, who bestowed a rich gift on me in return; and, having made some advantageous purchases, I arrived at Balsora, where, after I had sold my goods, I found myself possessed of a hundred thousand sequins.

## THE SECOND VOYAGE

Becoming weary of a quiet life in Balsora, and having purchased commodities, I again went to sea with some merchants. After having touched at several places, we landed at an uninhabited island. We amused ourselves in different ways, but I, having taken my wine and provisions, sat down and fell asleep. When I awoke, I found that my companions were gone, and that the ship had sailed. I climbed to the top of a very high tree, and perceived at a distance an object that was very large and white. I descended to the ground, and ran towards this strange-looking object. When I approached it I found it was about fifty paces in circumference, quite round, and as smooth as ivory, but had no sort of opening. It was now almost sunset, and suddenly the sky became darkened. I looked up and beheld a bird of enormous size, moving like a prodigious cloud towards me. I recollected that I had heard of a bird called the roc, so large that it could carry away young elephants, and I therefore conjectured that the large object I had been looking at was the egg of this bird.

As the bird approached I crept close to the egg, so that I had one of the legs of this winged animal before me; this limb being as large as the trunk of a tree, I tied myself firmly to it with my turban.

The next morning the bird flew away, and carried me from this desert island. I was borne so high that I could not see the earth, and then carried downwards so swiftly that I lost my senses. When I recovered, finding myself on the ground, I quickly untied the cloth that bound me, and scarcely was I free, when the bird, having taken up a large serpent, again flew away. I found myself in a deep valley, the sides of which were too steep to be ascended. As I walked up and down in despair, I perceived that the valley was strewed with diamonds of surprising magnitude. But I soon saw other objects of much less inviting appearance. Serpents of the most terrific size were peeping out of holes on every side. When night came, I took shelter in a cave, the entrance of which I guarded with the largest stones I could find, but the hissing of the serpents entirely deprived me of sleep. When day returned, the serpents retired to their holes; and I came out of my cave, but with extreme fear. I walked heedless of the serpents until I became weary, and then

sat down and fell asleep. I was awakened by something which fell near me. It was a large piece of fresh meat, and presently I saw several other pieces.

I was now convinced that I must be in the famous valley of diamonds, and that the pieces of meat were thrown in by merchants, who expected eagles to pounce upon the flesh, to which diamonds were almost sure to adhere. I hastened to pick up some of the largest diamonds I could find, which I put into a little bag, and fastened it to my girdle. I then selected the largest piece of flesh in the valley, which I tied to my waist with the cloth of my turban, and then lay down upon my face to wait for the eagles. Very soon one of the strongest pounced upon the meat on my back, and flew with me to its nest on the top of the mountain. The merchants began shouting to frighten the eagles, and when they had obliged the birds to quit their prey, one of them came to the nest where I was. At first the man was frightened when he saw me there, but having recovered himself, asked me how

SINDBAD FINDS THE SERPENTS

I came hither. I told him and the rest of the merchants my story. I then opened my bag, and they declared that they had never seen diamonds of equal lustre and size with mine. The merchants having gathered their diamonds together, we left the place the next morning; and crossed the mountains until we reached a port. We there took shipping and proceeded to the island of Roha. There I exchanged some of my diamonds for other merchandise, and we proceeded to Balsora. From Balsora I proceeded to my native city, Bagdad, in which I lived in ease upon the vast riches I had acquired.

## THE THIRD VOYAGE

I soon resolved upon a third voyage, and once more took shipping at Balsora. After we had been at sea a few weeks, we were overtaken by a dreadful storm, and were obliged to cast anchor near an island which the captain had endeavoured to avoid; for he assured us that it was inhabited by pigmy savages, covered with hair, who would speedily attack us in great numbers. Soon an innumerable multitude of frightful savages, about two feet high, boarded the ship. Resistance was useless. They took down our sails, cut our cable, towed the ship to land, and made us all go on shore. We went towards the interior of the island and discovered a large building. It was a lofty palace, having a gate of ebony, which we pushed open, and soon discovered an apartment in which were human bones and roasting spits. Presently there appeared a hideous black man, who was as tall as a palm tree. He had but one eye, his teeth were long and sharp, and his nails like the talons of a bird. He took me up as I would a kitten, but finding I was little better than skin and bone, put me down with disdain. The captain, being the fattest of the party, was sacrificed to his appetite. When the monster had finished his meal he stretched himself upon a great stone bench in the portico, and fell asleep, snoring louder than thunder. In this manner he slept till morning. In the morning he went out. I said to my companions:

"Do not waste time in useless sorrow; let us hasten to look for timber to make rafts."

We found some timber on the seashore, and laboured hard; but having no tools, it was evening before we had finished; and whilst we were on the point of pushing the raft off the beach, our hideous tyrant returned and drove us to his palace, as if we had been a flock of sheep. We saw another of our companions sacrificed, and the giant lay down to sleep as before. Our desperate condition gave us courage; nine of us got up very softly, and held the points of the roasting spits in the fire until we made them red-hot; we then thrust them at once into the monster's eye. He uttered a frightful scream, and having endeavoured in vain to find us, opened the ebony gate and left the palace. We did not stay long behind him, but hastened to the seashore, and having got our rafts ready, only waited for daylight to embark. But at dawn we beheld our monstrous enemy, led by two giants of equal size, and followed by many others. We jumped upon our rafts, and pushed them from the shore, the tide assisting us. The giants seeing us likely to escape, tore great pieces of rock, and wading in the water up to their waists, hurled them at us with all their might. They sunk every one of the rafts but that on which I was; thus all my companions, excepting two, were drowned. We rowed as fast as we could, and got out of the reach of these monsters. We were at sea two days, but at last found a pleasant island. Having eaten some fruit, we lay down to sleep, but were soon awakened by the hissing of an enormous serpent. One of my comrades was instantly devoured by this terrific creature. I climbed up a tree as fast as I could, and reached the topmost branches; my remaining companion was following me, but the dreadful reptile entwined itself round the tree and caught him. The serpent then descended and glided away. I waited until late the next day before I ventured to descend. Evening again approached, and I gathered together a great quantity of small wood, brambles, and thorns. Having made them into faggots, I formed a circle round the tree, and fastened the uppermost to the branches of the tree. I then ascended to the highest branches. At night the serpent came again, but could not reach the tree; and having ineffectually gone round and round my little fortification until daylight, he went away. The next day I beheld a ship in full sail at a considerable distance. With the linen of my turban I made a signal, which was perceived. I was taken on board the ship and there related

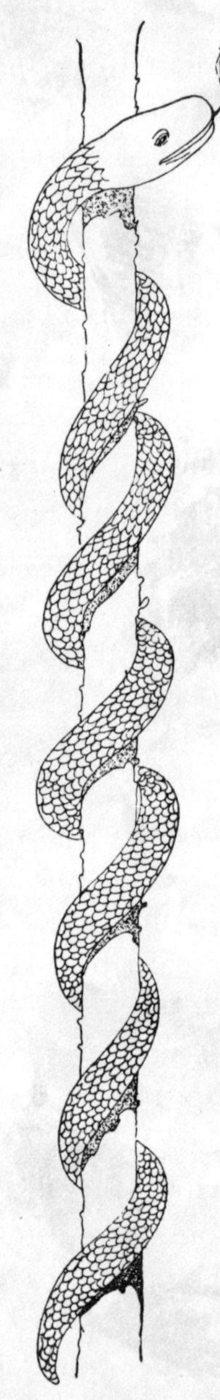

my adventures. The captain was kind in the extreme, and told me that he had some bales of goods which had belonged to a merchant who had unintentionally left him some time ago on an uninhabited island; and who, being unavoidably dead, he intended to sell the goods for the benefit of his relatives, and that I should have the profit of selling them. I now recollected this was the captain with whom I had sailed on my second voyage. I soon convinced him that I was really Sindbad, whom he supposed to have been lost. He was delighted at the discovery, and eagerly acknowledged that the property was mine. I continued my voyage, sold my goods to great advantage, and returned to Bagdad.

## THE FOURTH VOYAGE

My desire of seeing foreign countries rendered my pleasures at home perfectly unsatisfactory. I therefore arranged my affairs, commenced a voyage overland to Persia, and, having bought a large stock of goods, loaded a ship and again embarked. The ship struck upon a rock, and the cargo was lost. A few others and myself were borne by the current to an island, in which we were surrounded by black savages, and carried to their habitations. The savages offered us herbs; my companions eagerly took them, for they were hungry. Grief would not allow me to eat; and presently I perceived that the herbs had deprived my comrades of their senses. Rice, mixed with oil of cocoanuts, was then offered to us, of which my companions ate greedily. My unhappy friends were devoured one after another, having by these means become desirable to the cannibals. But I languished so much, that they did not think me fit to be eaten. They left me to the care of an old man, from whom I contrived to escape; and taking care to pursue a contrary way from that which the savages had gone I never stopped till night. At the end of seven days, on the seashore I found a number of white persons gathering pepper. They asked me in Arabic who I was, and whence I came; and I gave them an account of the shipwreck, and of my escape. They treated me kindly and presented me to their King, who behaved to me with great liberality. During my stay with them, I observed that when the King and his nobles went hunting, they rode their horses without bridle or saddle. With the assistance of some workmen I made a bridle and saddle, and having put them upon one of the King's horses, presented the animal thus accoutred to His Majesty. He was so delighted, that he instantly mounted and rode about the grounds almost the whole day. All the ministers of state and the nobility induced me to make saddles and bridles for them, for which they made me such magnificent presents that I soon became extremely rich. The King at last re-

quested that I would marry, and become one of his nation. From a variety of circumstances I could not refuse, and he therefore gave me one of the ladies of his Court, who was young, rich, beautiful, and virtuous. We lived in the greatest harmony in a palace belonging to my wife. I had contracted a great intimacy with a very worthy man who lived in this place. Having heard one day that his wife had just died, I hastened to condole with him on this unexpected calamity. We were alone together, and he appeared to be in the deepest grief. After I had remonstrated with him some time on the inutility of so much sorrow, he told me that it was an established law that the living husband should be buried with the deceased wife, and that within an hour he must submit. I shuddered at the dreadful custom. In a short time the woman was attired in her most costly dress and jewels, and placed in an open coffin. The procession then began, the husband following the corpse. They ascended to the top of an exceedingly high mountain, and a great stone was removed, which covered the mouth of a deep pit. The corpse was let down, and the husband, having taken leave of his friends, was put into another open coffin, with a pot of water and seven small loaves, and he was let down. The stone was replaced, and they all returned. The horror of this was still fresh upon my mind, when my wife fell sick and died. The King and the whole Court, out of respect to me, instantly prepared to assist at a similar ceremony with me. I restrained the feeling of despair until we arrived at the top of the mountain, when I fell at the feet of the King and besought him to spare my life. All I said was ineffectual, and after my wife was interred, I also was put down into the deep pit, all being totally indifferent to my cries and lamentations. I made the cave echo with my unavailing complaints. I lived some days on the bread and water which had been put into my coffin, but this supply was at length exhausted. I then wandered to a remote part of this frightful cave, and lay down to prepare for death. I was thus wishing only for a speedy termination to my misery, when I heard something walking and panting. I started up, upon which the thing panted still more, and then ran away. I pursued it, and sometimes it seemed to stop, but on my approach continued to go on before me. I pursued it, until at last I saw a glimmering light like a star. This redoubled my eagerness, until at last I discovered a hole large enough to allow my escape. I crept through the aperture, and found myself on the seashore, and discovered that the creature was a sea monster which had been accustomed to enter at that hole to feed upon the dead bodies. Having eaten some shellfish, I returned to the cave, where I collected all the jewels I could find in the dark. These I carried to the seashore, and having tied them up very neatly into bales with the cords that let down the coffins, I laid them on the beach, waiting till some ship should pass. In two days a ship came out of the harbour, and passed by that part of the coast. I made a signal, and a boat took me on board. I was obliged to say that I had been wrecked; for, had they known my real story, I should have been carried back, as the captain was a native of this country, We touched at several islands, and at the port of Kela, where I found a ship ready to sail for Balsora; and having presented some jewels to the captain who had brought me to Kela, I sailed, and at last arrived at Bagdad.

## THE FIFTH VOYAGE

Having forgotten my former perils, I built a ship at my own expense, loaded it with a rich cargo, and, taking with me other merchants, once more set sail. After having been much driven about by a storm, we landed upon a desert island to search for fresh water; we there found a roc's egg, equal in size to that which I had seen before. The merchants and sailors gathered round it, and though I advised them not to meddle with it, they nevertheless made a hole in it with their hatchets, and picked out the young roc, piece after piece, and roasted it. They had scarcely finished when two of the old birds appeared in the air. We hastened on board ship and set sail. We had not proceeded far before we saw the immense birds approaching us, and soon after they hovered over the ship. One of them let fall an enormous fragment of stone, which fell into the sea close beside the ship, but the other let fall a fragment which split our ship. I caught hold of a piece of the wreck, on which I was borne by the wind and tide to an island, the shore of which was very steep. I reached the dry land, and having found the most delicious fruits and excellent water, became refreshed. Farther in the island I saw a feeble old man sitting near a rivulet. When I enquired of him how he came thither, he only answered by signs for me to carry him over the rivulet, that he might eat some fruit. I took him on my back, and crossed the brook, but instead of getting down, he clasped his legs so firmly round my throat, that I thought he would have strangled me, so that with pain and fright I soon fainted. When I recovered, the old fellow was still in his former position, and he quickly made me rise up and walk under the trees, while he gathered the fruit at his ease. This lasted a considerable time. One day, while carrying him about, I picked up a large gourd called a calabash, and, having cleared out the inside, I pressed into it the juice of grapes. Having filled it, I left it for several days, and at length found that it became excellent wine. I drank of this, and for a while forgot my sorrows, so that I began to sing with cheerfulness. The old man made me give him the calabash, and liking the flavour of the wine, he drank it off, soon became intoxicated, fell from my

shoulders, and died in convulsions. I hastened to the seaside, and soon found the crew of a ship. They told me I had fallen into the hands of the Old Man of the Sea, and was the first person that had ever escaped. I sailed with them, and the captain, when we landed, took me to some persons whose employment was to gather cocoanuts. We all took up stones and pelted the monkeys that were at the very top of the cocoanut trees, and these animals in return pelted us with cocoanuts. When we had obtained as many as we could carry, we returned to the town. I soon obtained a considerable sum by the cocoanuts I thus obtained, and at length sailed for my native land.

## THE SIXTH VOYAGE

At the expiration of another year, I prepared ror a sixth voyage. This proved very long and unfortunate, for the pilot lost his course and knew not where to steer. At length he told us we must inevitably be dashed to pieces against a rock which we were fast approaching. In a few moments the vessel was a complete wreck. We saved our lives, our provisions, and our goods.

The shore on which we were cast was at the foot of a mountain which it was impossible to climb, so that I shortly beheld my companions die one after another. There was a frightful cavern in the rock, through which flowed a river. To this, in a fit of desperation, I resolved to trust myself. I went to work and made a long raft. I loaded it with bales of rich stuffs, and large pieces of rock crystal, of which the mountain was in a great measure formed. I went on board the raft, and the current carried me along. I was carried in darkness during many days, and at last fell asleep. When I awoke, I found myself in a pleasant country. My raft was tied up, and some blacks, who were near me, said that they had found me floating in the river which waters their land. They took me to their king, and carefully conducted my cargo with me. When we came to the city of Serindib, I related my story to the monarch, who ordered it to be written

in letters of gold. I presented the King with some of the most beautiful pieces of rock crystal, and entreated him to let me return to my own country, which he readily agreed to, and even gave me a letter and a present to my sovereign, the Caliph Haroun Alraschid. The present consisted of a ruby made into a cup, and decorated with pearls; the skin of a serpent, which appeared like burnished gold, and which could repel disease; some aloe-wood, camphire, and a female slave of excessive beauty. I returned to my native country, delivered the present to the Caliph, and received his thanks, with a reward.

## THE SEVENTH AND LAST VOYAGE

The Caliph Haroun Alraschid one day sent for me, and told me I must bear a present to the King of Serindib. I ventured to expostulate with him on account of my age, but I could not prevail on him to forgo his request. I arrived at Serindib, and prayed an audience with the King. I was conducted to the palace with great respect, and delivered to the monarch the Caliph's letter and present. The present consisted of the most ingenious and valuable works of art, with which the King was exceedingly delighted, and he was also pleased to acknowledge how much he esteemed my services. When I departed, the monarch bestowed on me some rich gifts; but the ship had not long been at sea, before it was attacked by corsairs, who seized the vessel, and carried us away as slaves. I was sold to a merchant, who, having found that I could use the bow and arrow with skill, took me upon an elephant, and carried me to a vast forest in the country. My master desired me to climb an exceedingly high tree, and wait there until I saw a troop of elephants pass by. I was then to shoot at them, and if one of them fell, I was to go to the city and give the merchant notice. Having given me these directions, and a bag of provisions, he left me. On the morning of the second day, I saw a great number of elephants. I succeeded in shooting one of them, upon which the others went away, and I returned to the city and told my employer; he commended my diligence and caressed me. We went back to the forest and dug a hole, in which the elephant was to remain until it decayed and left the teeth. I continued this trade nearly two months, and killed an elephant almost every day. One morning all the elephants came up to the tree in which I was; they howled dreadfully. One of them fastened his trunk round the tree and tore it up by the roots. I fell with the tree; the animal took me up with his trunk, and placed me on his back, and then, at the head of his troop, he brought me to a place where he gently laid me on the ground, and they all went away. I discovered that I was upon a large broad hill, covered all over with the bones and teeth of elephants, and was soon convinced that this was their burying-place. I reached the city once more; my master thought I was lost, for he had seen the torn tree, and found my bow and arrows. I told him what had happened, and conducted him to the hill. We loaded the elephant on which we had come, and thus collected more teeth than a man could have obtained in his whole life.

The merchant told me that not only he himself, but the whole city, was indebted to me, and that I should return to my own country with sufficient wealth to make me happy. My patron loaded a ship with ivory, and the other merchants made me valuable presents. I reached Balsora and landed my ivory, which I found to be much more valuable than I had expected. I set out with caravans to travel overland, and at last reached Bagdad, where I presented myself to the Caliph, and gave an account of my embassy. He was so astonished at my adventure with the elephants that he ordered the narrative of it to be written in letters of gold and to be deposited in his treasury.